Stories from Islam

Ibrahim's Sacrifice

Ziya Us Salam

An imprint of Om Books International

Rasheeda was reading the newspaper when she saw her grandson approaching her. She lowered her glasses and smiled at him fondly. “Yes, Salman, is there something that you want?” Her eyes twinkled. She knew what her grandson would ask for.

“You said you will tell me a story after you had finished reading the paper, Grandma,” Salman reminded his grandmother.

Rasheeda burst out laughing. “So I did. Well, I haven’t finished reading the paper, but I will tell you a story anyway. Today, Salman, you will listen to the story of Prophet Ibrahim. But first you must promise to be obedient to your parents.”

Salman gave his usual promise. "Why do you always make me give you the same promise, Grandma?" Salman asked his grandmother.

“I will tell you,” Rasheeda told Salman and began the tale, “Prophet Ibrahim was 87 years old when Allah blessed him with a son. Ibrahim brought up his children with a lot of love and care. He wanted them to be good human beings, who were obedient to Allah.

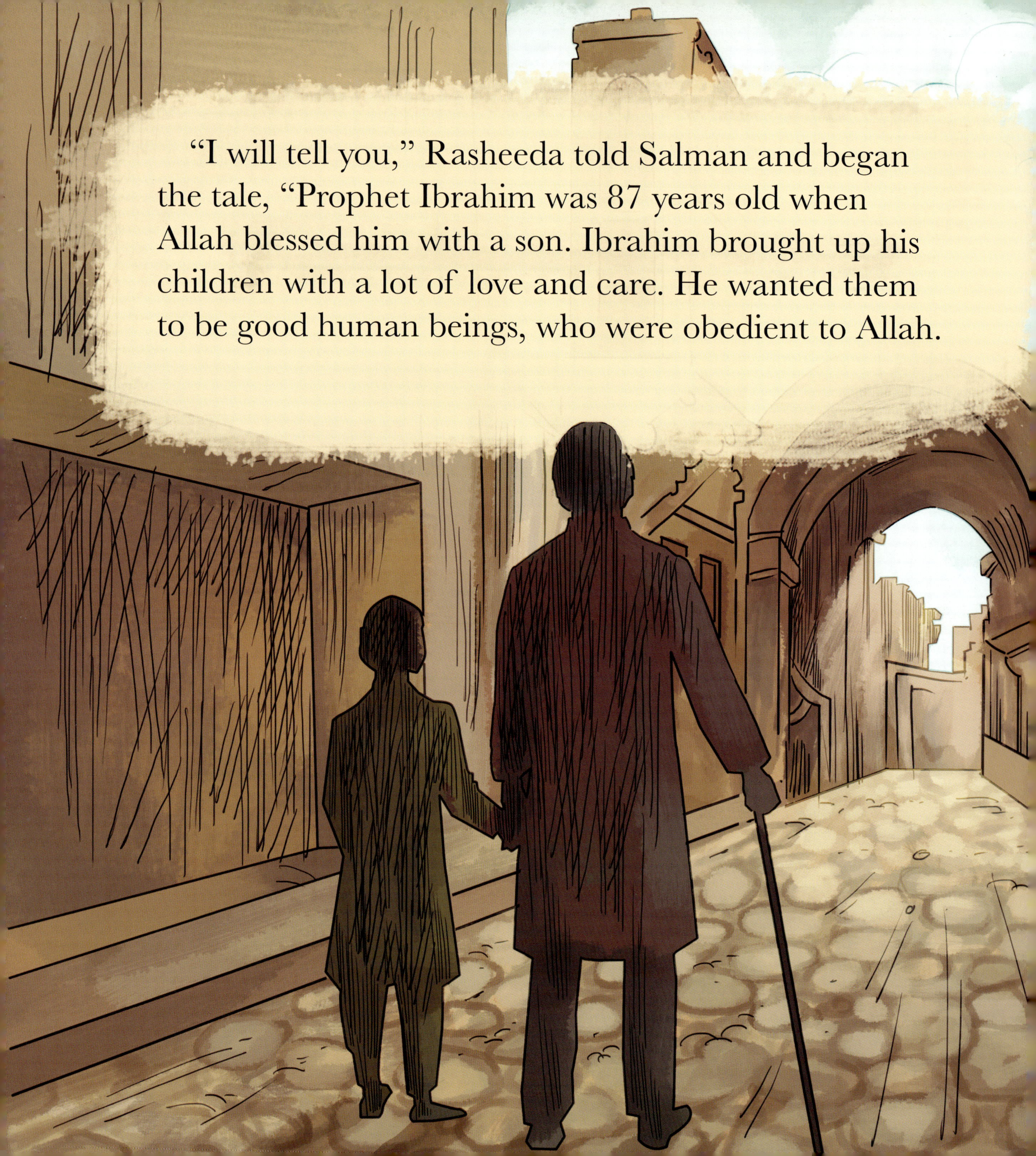

“Among his children was a boy, Ismail. One night, Ibrahim had a strange dream. He dreamt that Allah asked him to sacrifice Ismail! Prophet Ibrahim took his dream to be the work of Shaitan and ignored it. However, he had the same dream the next night, too. He realised then that Allah wanted him to sacrifice his beloved son.

"Next morning, Prophet Ibrahim and Ismail began their journey towards Mount Arafat. Along the way, when they reached Mina, the Shaitan told Prophet Ibrahim not to sacrifice Ismail.

"But Prophet Ibrahim was determined to obey Allah's command. He proceeded with Ismail to Mount Arafat.

"Once they reached there, he told Ismail the purpose of their journey. Young Ismail was not scared and asked his father to carry out Allah's order, and tie his hands and legs. He also asked Ibrahim to blindfold himself as Ibrahim would not be able to see his son suffer.

“Prophet Ibrahim tied his son’s hands and legs, and blindfolded himself. Then...”

“Then he sacrificed his son?” Salman asked in a hushed voice. He did not want Ismail to be sacrificed.

Rasheeda continued, "Prophet Ibrahim covered his eyes with a blindfold and used the knife. When he opened his eyes, Ismail stood there, unharmed! In place of Ismail, a ram lay dead. Suddenly, Prophet Ibrahim heard a voice, 'Allah looks after His creations.' Allah had been testing Prophet Ibrahim, and he had passed the test."

"So, Salman," Rasheeda folded the paper neatly. "Every year when people go for Hajj, they go to Mount Arafat as part of the pilgrimage. At Mina, they stone the Shaitan because he had tried to mislead Prophet Ibrahim there. People sacrifice an animal to remember the sacrifice of Prophet Ibrahim."

"I see," said Salman.

"Yes, you see, now?" smiled Rasheeda. "Will you remember your promise? Never disobey your parents. Remember how Prophet Ismail obeyed his father and passed the test!"